PR
for ev

by

JOSEPHINE AND
CHRISTOPHER BUNCH

The Canterbury Press
Norwich

A few days after completing the manuscript of this book of prayers Christopher died very suddenly and very peacefully. The family therefore dedicates this book to his memory.

We believe we have given him back to you dear God, who gave him to us. Yet as you did not lose him in giving so we have not lost him by his return. We thank you for every remembrance of him – his compassion and kindness; his quiet strength and dependable wisdom; his sheer goodness and his dedication and caring for all those you committed to his charge. We leave him in your keeping, thankful indeed for all that was of Christ in his character. To know him was to love him.

Christopher Bunch: Curate Lambeth 1938–41; P-in-C St Barnabas, Downham 1941–43; Chaplain R.N.V.R. 1943–46; V of Holy Trinity, Bromley Common 1946–56; V of Otford 1956–1984.

Take time to THINK . . .
It is the source of power.
Take time to PLAY . . .
It is the secret of perpetual youth.
Take time to READ . . .
It is the fountain of wisdom.
Take time to PRAY . . .
It is the greatest power on earth.
Take time to LOVE and BE LOVED . . .
It is a God-given privilege.
Take time to BE FRIENDLY . . .
It is the road to happiness.
Take time to LAUGH . . .
It is the music of the soul.
Take time to GIVE . . .
It is too short to be selfish.
Take time to WORK . . .
It is the price of success.
Take time to DO CHARITY . . .
It is the key to heaven.

(Anonymous, found on a bookmark)

The Lord's unfailing love and mercy still continue,
Fresh as the morning, as sure as the sunrise.
The Lord is all I have and so I put my hope in him.
Lamentations 3.22–24

1st MORNING

Jesus rose from the table, took off his outer garment and tied a towel round his waist. Then he poured some water into a basin and began to wash the disciples' feet and dry them with the towel round his waist.

St John 13. 4, 5

Service

Give us, dear Lord, the desire to live useful and not useless lives. Show us ways in which we can serve in the fellowship of your Church. Increase our love for you that we may grow in our witness of the Gospel and our understanding of the Faith. Strengthen us that we may be loving and caring to those in need, dedicating ourselves anew in your service.   Amen.

The Example of Jesus Christ

Lord, in you we have the perfect example of the way we ought to live. You showed your humility in the work of a carpenter; your gentleness in forgiving sinners; your kindness as you healed the sick and suffering; your love and compassion in your dealings with others. As we strive to grow more like you, fill us with your Holy Spirit, that we may have the courage and the strength to overcome our faults and failings and the diligence to seek you and find you, our Lord and Saviour. Amen.

Our Father . . .

> I have set an example for you, so that you will do just what I have done for you . . .Now that you know this truth, how happy you will be if you put it into practice.
>
> *St John 13. 15, 17*

1st EVENING

Love must be completely sincere. Hate what is evil, hold on to what is good.

Romans 12. 9

Confession

O God, we confess that today has been like so many other days.

We have ignored opportunities when we could have been helpful;
We have wasted chances to show kindness;
We have said things which would have been better left unsaid;
We have shown an uncaring attitude in situations which we should have tried hard to rectify.

We know too that we are sometimes guilty of jealous and envious thoughts and we do not always drive from our minds things that are dishonest and impure.

We ask you to cleanse us from all our sins and to grant us your forgiveness – the forgiveness promised to us through the sacrifice of your beloved Son upon the Cross.   Amen.

Families

Dear Lord, we ask your blessing on our family that each member of it may grow in love, unselfishness, thoughtfulness and gratitude. As we remember your home at Nazareth and wonder at the loving devotion of Mary and Joseph to you, inspire us with this same commitment to live our lives forgetful of self in our endeavour to create a Christ-centred home. And may we always be aware that we are members too of another family – that great army of Christians throughout the world – as we strive to do your will. This we ask in the name of Jesus Christ our Lord. Amen.

Our Father . . .

Serve the Lord with a heart full of devotion. Let your hope keep you joyful, be patient in your troubles, and pray at all times.

Romans 12. 11, 12

$2nd$ MORNING

> So then, you must clothe yourselves with compassion, kindness, humility, gentleness and patience.
>
> *Colossians 3. 12*

Kindness

O Lord Jesus, you always had time to be kind. We pray that you will help us to grow in kindness. Guard us from all envy and bitterness, and save us from thinking evil rather than good of another's intentions. Grant that we may never do a kind action in an unkind way and may always be quick with words of appreciation. Teach us to treat others as we would wish to be treated ourselves and especially, help us to remember the lonely, the shy and all who find it hard to mix with other people.   Amen.

Human Rights

We bring into your presence, God, all those who are suffering at this time through persecution and oppression; hostages who have been seized for political or other reasons; people who suffer because of the colour of their skin and all who are imprisoned unjustly. Touch the hearts of their captors with your love and compassion so that all those wrongfully deprived of their liberty, may be released and may once more know the joy of living in freedom. This we ask for your sake.   Amen.

Our Father . . .

> To all these qualities add love, which binds all things together in perfect unity.
>
> *Colossians 3. 14*

2nd EVENING

Well, whatever you do, whether you eat or drink, do it all for God's glory.

1 Corinthians 10. 31

Over-indulgence

Heavenly Father, we know so well the ills and evils which accompany over-indulgence.

From eating and drinking too much – forgive us, Lord.

From spending more than we ought – forgive us, Lord.

From spoiling those we love – forgive us, Lord.

From leading others into sin through our greed, our lust and our selfishness – forgive us, Lord.

From deliberately using our spare time to do just what we want to do – forgive us, Lord.

Help us to control our appetites and our desires that we may never forget that our greed and lack of discipline can harm the lives of others. This we ask for Christ's sake.   Amen.

Workers at Night

Dearest Lord, as we go to rest tonight, we pray for all who will work while we sleep. Comfort and cheer them in the loneliness of the night watches and give to each one of them encouragement and a sense of purpose as they go about their duties. When their work is done, grant them rest and refreshment and may we never take for granted those who keep the wheels of life turning while we sleep. This we pray through Jesus Christ our Lord.   Amen.

Our Father . . .

> Just do as I do; I try to please everyone in all that I do, not thinking of my own good, but of the good of all, so that they might be saved. Imitate me, then, just as I imitate Christ.
>
> *1 Corinthians 10. 33; 11. 1*

3rd MORNING

I have learnt this secret, so that anywhere, at any time, I am content.

Philippians 4. 12 (part)

Contentment

O Lord Jesus Christ, the light and hope of the world, free us from the fetters of discontent. Save us from grumbling which spoils so much of the happiness of our everyday life and fails to recognise the richness and variety of this wonderful world in which we live. Give us the strength and the will to triumph over all feelings of resentment and frustration. Fill our lives with the serenity and peace which flow from a firm faith in you and surround us with your love which is the same yesterday, today and forever.

Our Friends

Teach us, Lord, to value our friendships. Grant that we may never ignore the friendly smile, the handshake, the touch of a loved one, the encouraging word or the sympathetic understanding of those closest to us. May we always appreciate the help and support which our friends give us, and even if they have to criticise us, may we remember that they are doing this for our own good. O Lord, the friend of the outcast and the sinner, we pray that we may always try to be a friend to all we meet – even as you are the best and truest friend of all those who put their trust in you. Amen.

Our Father . . .

> A person who obeys God in everything and always does what is right, whose words are true and sincere and who does not slander others, he does no wrong to his friends, and does not spread rumours about his neighbours.
>
> *Psalm 15. 2, 3*

3rd EVENING

How dare you say to your brother, Please, let me
take that speck out of your eye, when you have a
log in your own eye? You hypocrite! First take the
log out of your own eye and then you will be able
to see clearly to take the speck out of your brother's
eye.

St Matthew 7. 4, 5

Hypocrisy

Forgive us, Lord, for the times when we have
looked at or listened to things which make us
ashamed;
for the idle words we speak which could be
describing ourselves and which, instead, damage
or destroy the character of another;
for the unkind criticism which first refuses to see
the plank in our own eye;
for every occasion when we could have taken
action but have ignored opportunities to speak up
for what is right;
for our lack of honesty and our selfishness which
we readily condemn in others.

Please help us to overcome any form of hypocrisy
in our own lives, dearest Lord, before we find
fault with others.   Amen.

Radio and Television

We thank you Lord for giving us the chance to share in so many aspects of life through radio and television. Up to the minute news is brought to us as it is actually happening and we see a mixture of programmes which stagger us by their diversity. We pray that as we look and listen, the many choices of programmes confronting us may raise and not lower our moral standards; and that all those involved in public speaking and appearing on television may use their talents in a responsible way, remembering the power for good which the media affords them as opposed to the power of evil which generates corrupting influences. This we ask for Jesus' sake.   Amen.

Our Father . . .

> Fill your minds with those things that are good and that deserve praise; things that are true, noble, right, pure, lovely and honourable.
>
> *Philippians 4. 8*

4th MORNING

I will always guide you and satisfy you with good things.

Isaiah 58. 11

Guidance

God our Father, we ask you to rule our lives and to guide us in your ways. Strengthen our wills and give us wisdom to see how we can serve you better. Fill our lives with your Holy Spirit that we may have the power to overcome temptations and to grow in understanding and godliness. Direct our thinking and prosper our endeavours that we may do what is well pleasing in your sight, and as we seek your will, teach us how to live. This we ask for the sake of him who died for us, Jesus Christ our Lord. Amen.

Leaders in Church and State

Almighty God, king and judge of all mankind, we pray for those men and women holding the great responsibility of high office in Church and State. Surround them with your love and dispel from their lives harmful ambition, unfair judgements and hostile acts which can result in bitterness and strife. Enfold them in your ways and keep ever before them the inspiration of your perfect leadership, that their decisions may make for true and lasting peace based on goodwill and justice. Amen.

Our Father . . .

> We urge you, to warn the idle, encourage the timid, help the weak, be patient with everyone.
>
> *1 Thessalonians 5. 14*

4th EVENING

Do not let evil defeat you; instead, conquer evil with good.

Romans 12. 21

Ill Will

O King of Kings, shed your light into the dark corners of the world. Where there is discord bring understanding and where there is ill will bring the healing powers of your love. Give us a firm trust in you that we may shun all feelings of revenge, learning to forgive those who anger and annoy us and entrusting them to your care and keeping. When we are feeling cross and irritable, may we remind ourselves of all the blessings we so richly enjoy, that we may be thankful for what we have and ready to share with those who have so little but who complain far less than we do ourselves. This we ask in Jesus' name.   Amen.

Transport

O God, who has put into our hands the power to travel at great speeds by land and sea and air, fill us with a desire to use the roads, the sea and the airways with courtesy and consideration for others. Teach us to practice thoughtfulness, that we may not knowingly increase the risk of accident or injury by our carelessness or selfishness. Make us watchful to help those in trouble or distress as they travel from place to place, always keeping before us the example of your dear Son, Our Lord, and his complete dedication to the wellbeing of others during his life on earth. So bring us all safely to our journeys' end.   Amen.

Our Father . . .

> The Lord will protect you from all danger; he will keep you safe. He will protect you as you come and go now and forever.
>
> *Psalm 121. 7, 8*

5th MORNING

Peter spoke up and said to Jesus 'I will never leave you, even though all the rest do!'

St Matthew 26. 33

Loyalty

Almighty God, whose Son in his days on earth remained true to duty, even unto the Cross, fill us with this same desire to be loyal in all things. Grant that we may show constancy and faithfulness befitting all who try to follow you. Teach us to give deference to those in authority over us, obedience to the laws of our land and fidelity to your holy will. May we never let down our family, our friends, our colleagues or our acquaintances by being disloyal and in all things, help us to strive for honesty and truth. This we ask for Jesus Christ's sake. Amen.

Daily Work

As we wake to meet another day, we thank you Lord for giving us the health and strength to do our daily work. Whether it be at school or college, home or office, shop or factory, or any other place where the business of daily living is carried on, give us the will to do our work to the best of our ability. We know that a job worth doing at all is worth doing well and we pray that however dull or monotonous or unspectacular our work may be, you will strengthen us to give of our best, ever conscious that you are the unseen Lord of our life and you know when we shirk or shelve our duties.

Our Father . . .

> Work hard at whatever you do.
>
> *Ecclesiastes 9. 10*

5th EVENING

Lazy people should learn a lesson from the way ants live.

Proverbs 6. 6

Laziness

It is so easy to be lazy Lord, and to put off until tomorrow things which should have been done today.

It is so easy to stand by and watch as others, more willing than we are, get on with the job.

It is so easy to make excuses and not turn up when we had previously promised to help.

It is so easy to put pleasure before duty and getting before giving. Save us from living neglectful and careless lives and strengthen our sense of duty, that we may cheerfully accomplish those tasks which you have set us to do, ever conscious that this world is but a training ground for heaven. Amen.

Saints

We thank you God for those holy men and women who have lived their lives as Saints on earth – those who by their example and witness have pointed the way from earth to heaven. We think especially of those unknown Saints whose shining examples have inspired us to persevere in our times of doubt and lack of trust. Fill us with your Holy Spirit that we may be equipped to follow in their footsteps and so inherit, with them, the life of your eternal Kingdom, through Jesus Christ our Lord.   Amen.

Our Father . . .

> As for us, we have this large crowd of witnesses round us. So then, let us rid ourselves of everything that gets in the way, and of the sin which holds on to us so tightly, and let us run with determination the race that lies before us. Let us keep our eyes fixed on Jesus, on whom our faith depends from beginning to end.
>
> *Hebrews 12. 1 2*

6th MORNING

So Jesus said to those who believed in him, 'If you obey my teaching, you are really my disciples; you will know the truth and the truth will set you free'.
St John 8.31, 32

Truthfulness

Lord, in our search for the truth give us the determination to say what we mean and mean what we say. May our word be our bond and at all times may we speak the truth that no hopes or fears may lead us to act or speak falsely. We know that truthfulness is one of the hallmarks of a good Christian life, and that one small untruth may lead to another until we create a situation where lies take over from honesty. Keep us ever watchful not make statements before we have made sure they are true, and to keep silent if truthfulness will cause unnecessary distress. So we pray that You will be to us the way, the truth and the life.   Amen.

Knowledge

Almighty God, as you unfold the wonders of the world to us day by day, make us increasingly aware of the dangers of greed and selfishness. Alert us to the needs of those who will come after us, that future generations may reap the benefit of our knowledge and experience. We thank you Lord, for the great advances which have been made in the fields of medicine, science and technology and we pray that this knowledge may by used for the benefit of all people both now and in the years to come. This we ask for Christ's sake.   Amen.

Our Father . . .

> Give me wisdom and knowledge, because I trust in your commands.
>
> *Psalm 119.66*

6th EVENING

So then, you must never think that you have made yourselves wealthy by your own power and strength. Remember that it is the Lord your God who gives you the power to become rich.

Deuteronomy 8. 17, 18

Materialism

With so much emphasis on getting and spending Lord; it is sometimes hard to remember that the happiness and purpose of life depends far less on earthly possessions and the pleasures of this world, than upon heavenly gifts and the things of the spirit. Money cannot buy the smile of a baby, the love of our families, the sympathy of a friend or the example of a Saint. Too much money can make us avaricious, irreverent and uncaring, only thinking of ourselves and what we can get and have for our material comforts. Lord, help us to fix our hearts, our desires and our love upon you, and grant that in our daily living we may put you and our love for you before all else.   Amen.

Printed Matter

We think tonight Lord of all those who earn their livelihood by what they write. We pray that you will direct their hearts and minds away from any form of writing which will harm the reader, whether it be in novels, magazines or newspaper articles. Grant that those who write may not distort facts to make sensational reading. Encourage in them standards of living which will influence their lives and the lives of their readers for good; and, in their turn, we pray that readers may reject any printed matter which is vulgar or harmful and may choose to read only that which is acceptable in your sight, our Lord and our God.   Amen.

Our Father . . .

> A good man's words are like pure silver . . .A good man's words will benefit many people.
> *Proverbs 10. 20, 21*

7th MORNING

Peace is what I leave with you; it is my own peace that I give you. I do not give it as the world does. Do not be worried and upset; do not be afraid.

St John 14. 27

Serenity

As we begin another day, Lord, keep us serene no matter what troubles and difficulties we may have to face. Shine through our lives that others may see something of your peace and love reflected in us as we go about our daily business. Help us to ride out the storms of life with a firm trust in your unfailing protection, and fill us with your Holy Spirit, that whatever may befall us, nothing will separate us from you and your loving care for each one of us. Calm all who have to face the unknown today – those taking examinations; those being interviewed for a job; those who must undergo an operation; those who are frustrated by ill health or old age. Lord, pour upon them and us the peace which passes human understanding. This we ask in the name of the Prince of Peace, Jesus Christ our Lord.   Amen.

God's Word

O God our heavenly Father, we thank you for all the wisdom, teaching and instruction we can find in the Bible. Help us to study your word so that we can increase in our knowledge of our Lord, and, as we learn more about him may we increase in our love for him and be obedient to him. Bless all those occupied in translating the Bible into other languages, that more and more people in the world may have the chance to own a Bible written in their own language, and may find in its pages comfort in trouble, guidance in making right decisions and wisdom in difficulties. This we ask for Jesus Christ's sake.   Amen.

Our Father . . .

> All scripture is inspired by God, and is useful for teaching the truth, rebuking error, correcting faults, and giving instruction for right living, so that the person who serves God may be fully qualified and equipped to do every kind of good deed.
>
> *2 Timothy 3. 16*

7th EVENING

And the tongue is like a fire . . . We use it to give thanks to our Lord and Father and also to curse our fellow-man who is created in the likeness of God. Words of thanksgiving and cursing pour out from the same mouth. My Brothers, this should not happen.

James 3. 6 (part), 9 & 10

Harsh Words

Teach us, heavenly Father, to live in harmony with one another. Make us careful to think before we speak and to curb hasty judgements before it is too late; remembering our own faults and failings before we criticise others. We confess with sorrow all the harsh words we have said and the friends we have failed through undisciplined conversation. Incline our hearts to love and not condemn, that our tongues may be controlled and our speech sincere and kind, through Jesus Christ our Lord. Amen.

Broken Relationships

We bring into your presence, Lord, all those who are facing problems in their relationships with others.

Children who feel unloved and unwanted by their parents and parents who find their children hard to discipline and control.

Brothers and sisters who have fallen out with each other and so lost the love and companionship they once enjoyed.

Husbands and wives whose marriages have broken down and who are left bewildered and alone.

Those who are older, whose families have forsaken them and who feel unable to cope on their own any longer.

Teach us to see Lord that unkind or thoughtless actions can affect the lives of many more than just we ourselves, and help us to work at our relationships with others, that we may strive not to be the cause of broken or divided homes.   Amen.

Our Father . . .

Love one another earnestly with all your heart.
1 Peter 1. 22(b)

8th MORNING

Be alert, stand firm in the faith, be brave, be strong. Do all your work in love.

1 Corinthians 16. 13

Courage

Give us courage Lord

To stand up for the right;
To show self-control when we are tempted to sin;
To face the difficulties and dangers which confront us bravely;
Never to run away from situations where our help may be needed;
To be strong-minded in upholding the Christian way of life, even if this means that we are left in isolation;

We understand that standards are harder to uphold in an indulgent society, but we know too, Lord, that with your help we can face life in the knowledge that you will always be by our side. Hear our prayer and let our cry come unto you.   Amen.

Dangerous Occupations

We thank you, heavenly Father, for all those brave men and women who serve the community in dangerous occupations and for those who are prepared to risk their lives to preserve the safety of us all. We are sad to think that by the bad behaviour of the few, drug addiction, drunkenness and arson can cause so much heartbreak; and that in self-protection, bombs have to be defused and guns fired. Dear God, please help those who perpetrate these evil deeds to see that their actions can never bring anything but sadness and broken hearts, and grant that trouble-makers may be filled with a desire to seek reconciliation and forgiveness rather than revenge and retribution.   Amen.

Our Father . . .

> Put on all the armour that God gives you, so that you will be able to stand up against the Devil's evil tricks.
>
> *Ephesians 6. 11*

8th EVENING

So do not worry about tomorrow; it will have enough worries of its own. There is no need to add to the troubles each day brings.

St Matthew 6. 34

Worry

Many times, Lord, you showed us in your earthly life how trust in God can dispel our cares and ease our problems.
We recall –

how you used a boy's picnic to feed the five thousand;
how you slept in a boat, unconcerned, while a storm raged and only woke when you had to calm the fears of your disciples;
how, even on the Cross, in your agony, you remembered your mother and prayed for forgiveness for those who had treated you so cruelly.

We confess that we spoil our lives by worrying about things which never happen. We pray that walking hand in hand with you, we may know that assurance which comes to all who learn to commit their lives to God's care and keeping. Amen.

Homeless and Unemployed

We bring into your presence Lord those whose burdens are so much greater than our own.
We pray tonight for –

those who have no home, no place to call their own; especially the young homeless;
the unwanted and unloved;
those who have no work to do;
those who have taken on more borrowing than they can afford to pay back;
those for whom the future is bleak;
the despised and deprived in the poorer countries of the world.

Protect them from being exploited or imposed upon, and make us ready and eager to help those we meet who are less fortunate than we are ourselves. This we ask for Christ's sake.   Amen.

Our Father . . .

> The Lord lifts those who have fallen. He loves his righteous people. He protects the strangers who live in our land; He helps widows and orphans. The Lord heals the broken-hearted and bandages their wounds.
>
> *Psalm 146. 8b 9 and Psalm 147. 3*

9th MORNING

> Dear friends, let us love one another, because love comes from God. Whoever loves is a child of God and knows God. Whoever does not love does not know God, for God is love.
>
> *1 John 4. 7, 8*

Love

O God of love, inspire in us today and always a deeper understanding of true Christian love. May we remember that love means giving ourselves in the service of others; love is patient and kind, knows no jealousy, makes no parade, gives itself no airs, is never rude, selfish, irritated or resentful. Love is not glad when others go wrong, but love is gladdened by goodness, always eager to believe the best and always hopeful. May we never forget your greatest commands that we should love you with all our heart and soul and mind and our neighbours as ourselves, and may we never pause to consider the price we must pay to give the love we know we ought to give. This we ask for Jesus Christ's sake. Amen.

The Sick and Suffering

Most merciful Lord, we ask your blessing on all those who are sick in mind or body. Comfort and cheer them that they may have courage and fortitude as they face the pain and suffering laid upon them. We pray for the physically handicapped, for the deaf, dumb and blind; for those who have lost the power of reason and those whose pain is worse in the slow night hours. We remember especially those who are terminally ill and we give thanks for all doctors, nurses, relatives and friends who, by their devotion and skill, tend the needs of those committed to their care. Finally we pray that all who have to bear suffering of any kind (here remember any we know) may turn to you, Lord, for strength, encouragement and consolation.   Amen.

Our Father . . .

> When did we ever see you sick or in prison, and visit you? The King will reply, 'I tell you, whenever you did this for one of the least important of these brothers of mine, you did it for me!'
>
> *St Matthew 25. 39, 40*

9th EVENING

He died for all, so that those who live should no longer live for themselves, but only for Him who died and was raised to life for their sake.

2 Corinthians 5. 15

Selfishness

We thank you, heavenly Father, for all the things which give us so much pleasure in our lives – radio and television for our entertainment; games to play and music to enjoy; hobbies which can bring us many different interests, and books to read which open our minds to new thoughts and wider horizons. But these are all passing delights which we know can make us selfish and self-centred. Help us not to get our lives so full of the things we enjoy doing that we forget the needs of others – our families and friends – the visit to one who is ill or the forgotten letter which would mean so much to some lonely person. Keep before us the truth that selflessness demands sacrifice, thoughtfulness and a love of others, so bringing out the best in us. Forgive us God for the times when we have pleased ourselves to the detriment of others and encourage us to grow in unselfishness and concern for our fellow men and women, boys and girls.   Amen.

People of Other Lands

Dear God, we have received numerous blessings for which we should be very thankful, and so we pray for the countless people in the world whose lives are so much harder than our own. Tonight we think of those in other lands who live in poverty and degradation – coloured people who are rejected as inferior; those who are badly treated for their political views or who are imprisoned for their Christian beliefs. When we grumble about our own circumstances, help us to count our blessings and make us more ready to share the chances we have to learn about you and your love. This we ask in the name of Jesus Christ our Lord.   Amen.

Our Father . . .

> You did not despise or reject me. Instead you received me as you would an angel from Heaven. You received me as you would Christ Jesus.
>
> *Galatians 4. 14(b)*

10th MORNING

We have tested our brother many times and found him always very eager to help.

2 Corinthians 8. 22

Enthusiasm

Lord Jesus, we pray that we may capture some of that same spirit of infectious enthusiasm which filled your disciples on the first day of Pentecost. Give us the courage to speak up for you whenever we can, without adopting the pious attitude which can put people off their eagerness in their search for you. Make us careful never to dampen the ardour of anyone who is trying to uphold Christian standards, and deepen our concern wherever we see apathy or complacency. Increase our resolve to fight the evils of the world in the name of our blessed Lord and Saviour, Jesus Christ. Amen.

The Work of the Church

Rouse us, as members of your living Church, Lord, from within the confines of our church buildings and inspire us to take our Christian beliefs out into the world. Help us to see the great urgency of spreading your Gospel that wherever we go, we may use our lips to speak for you, our eyes to see where we can work for you, and our ears to hear when others need you. We pray for all who have dedicated their lives to your service. Give them courage and insight as they teach and preach and stir us to support missions at home and abroad through our prayers, our gifts and our deeds. So may we play our part in building your kingdom here upon earth. This we ask for Jesus Christ's sake.   Amen.

Our Father . . .

Set your heart on proclaiming God's message.

1 Corinthians 14. 39

10th EVENING

Have reverence for Christ in your hearts and honour him as Lord.

1 Peter 3. 15

Irreverance

We confess, almighty God, that sometimes we are guilty of profaning your holy name. We scoff and swear and blaspheme and we are not worthy to be called one of your followers. Forgive us Lord for this form of showing off; for using your name wrongly to impress others and for not giving you the reverence that only you deserve. Help us to grow in respect for those set in authority over us – our parents, our friends and all whom we love; and as we learn to understand how love and respect combine to show us the best way to treat others, may our love and adoration grow for you, our God and our King.   Amen.

Perseverance in Prayer

We pray Lord for ourselves, together with all those countless Christians throughout the world who truly believe that more things are wrought by prayer than this world dreams of. Guide us to pray for the right things supported by the right motives. Forgive us when our prayers are slipshod or hurried. Help us to be regular in our times of prayer, and when our prayers are not answered in the way we expect or want, make us content to abide your will for us, the one who knows all our needs even before we pray about them. This we ask for Jesus Christ's sake.   Amen.

Our Father . . .

> Be persistent in prayer, and keep alert as you pray, giving thanks to God.
>
> *Colossians 4. 2*

11th MORNING

See how patient a farmer is as he waits for his land to produce precious crops. He waits patiently for the autumn and spring rains. You also must be patient.

James 5. 7, 8

Patience

Help us, dear Lord, to grow in patience.

Give us patience in our dealings with others – especially with those whom we find it hard to like.

Give us patience to tackle a problem until it is solved without becoming irritable or annoyed.

Forgive our lack of patience –
With little children who tend to demand our full attention when we are tired or want to get on with something we had planned to do.

With those who are older and who find it hard to hurry or to react as quickly as they used to in speech and thought.

When we ourselves travel by land, sea or air, grant that we may never be responsible for any hasty action which may hurt or injure another.

This we ask in the name of our blessed Lord.   Amen.

Those Involved in Health Care

We pray this morning, Lord, for all those who devote their lives to the care of the sick and suffering;
for doctors and nurses who draw upon their knowledge and skill to make others well again;
for hospital staff who cook and clean, man transport and generally supply the needs of patients in their pain and discomfort;
for voluntary workers who so willingly give of their time to visit, supply books, run mobile shops and encourage and support any who need their help.

Lord, you showed your concern for the sick when you lived here on earth. Use us as instruments of your love that we may never neglect our duty to those who suffer, and grant that all those who bear the burden of sickness may know the peace which only you can give them, our Lord and our Saviour.   Amen.

Our Father . . .

> The trees will provide food and their leaves will be used for healing people.
>
> *Ezekiel 47. 12 (part)*

11th EVENING

Our great desire is that each one of you keep up his eagerness to the end, so that the things you hope for will come true. We do not want you to become lazy, but to be like those who believe and are patient, and so receive what God has promised.

Hebrews 6. 11, 12

Carelessness

Lord Jesus Christ, we confess with sadness how far we have fallen short of the standards you have set us.

We ask you to pardon –
Our careless treatment of any who stand in our way;
Our indifference to the needs of the world in our greed for earthly possessions;
Our neglect of your work in our church and neighbourhood and our feeble witness when we should have spoken up boldly for you;
Our wandering thoughts and inattention during our times of prayer;
Our lack of care in the way we use our time here on earth.

We pray that our resolve to serve you better may be strengthened, and that we may use the gifts you have given us more effectively, so that with your help we may live more useful lives.   Amen.

The Anxious and Bereaved

Almighty God, we beseech you to comfort all those who are in any kind of trouble. We remember those who are facing the worries of family life, the loneliness of a broken marriage, the illness of a loved one, the frustrations of bringing up a difficult or backward child. We pray for any who must sit by the bed of a loved one and wait for the end to come. We bring into your presence all those who have been bereaved and who do not know which way to turn in their sadness – especially parents who have lost a much-loved child. May we never pass by any needing our compassion, but always be ready to talk or to listen to any in distress, drawing upon the power of the Holy Spirit to guide us in all we say and do.   Amen.

Our Father . . .

We believe that Jesus died and rose again, and so we believe that God will take back with Jesus those who have died believing in him. So then encourage one another with these words.

1 Thessalonians 4. 14, 18

12th MORNING

> Stop judging by external standards, and judge by true standards.
>
> *St John 7. 24*

Right Judgement

Help us, Lord, to have a right judgement in all things.

To speak what is true and reject what is false;
To see what is good and shun what is evil;
To be honest in our dealings with others, so spurning deceit and insincerity;
To be careful not to overspend on ourselves and to be ready to give help to just causes;
To be fair in passing opinions and unwilling to agree with unkind and unfounded criticisms.

Make us eager to walk in your ways, that we may increase in integrity and not stumble into the many pitfalls of life as we try to do your will. This we ask for Christ's sake.   Amen.

Family Unity

Almighty God and Father of us all, we pray for the unity of each and every family. Where there is conflict bring harmony, and where there is mistrust and misunderstanding bring love and forgiveness, that happy family life may be the cornerstone on which society is built. Bless all children in the care of their parents, and bless all parents that they may realise the great responsibility you have laid upon them in bringing up their children. Bless brothers and sisters that they may be loyal and loving and the extended family, that grandparents and great grandparents, aunts and uncles, nephews and nieces, may all play their part in stimulating the togetherness of earthly family life – ever turning to the perfect pattern of your dear Son, Jesus Christ, who, from a lowly carpenter's son became the Saviour of the world. Amen.

Our Father . . .

> But if we live in the light – just as he is in the light – then we have fellowship with one another, and the blood of Jesus, his Son, purifies us from every sin.
> *1 John 1. 7*

12th EVENING

Jesus said 'There were ten men who were healed, where are the other nine? Why is this foreigner the only one who came back to give thanks to God?'

St Luke 17. 17, 18

Ingratitude

Lord, we confess our lack of gratitude for this wonderful world in which we live; for the air we breathe and the food we eat; for the seasons in all their beauty and variety; for the love and devotion of those who supply our daily needs; for sleep and rest and a home to go to when night comes; for friends to share our joys and sorrows. Dear Lord, our blessings are endless for there is so much you have given us, and yet we hear the song of a bird without listening, or see the glories of the sky at sunset without so much as a backward glance. Forgive us for our lack of appreciation and make us more grateful for our life, our health, and above all else for you and your love for each one of us. Amen.

Depression

Help us, Lord, to overcome our fits of depression. When black clouds and seemingly insoluble problems threaten us, strengthen us in our resolve to meet them with courage and confidence. We confess that sometimes we let despondency take over our lives and we forget that our depression increases unless we fight it from within ourselves. Deliver us from minds and thoughts which can only add to our gloom and distress. Create in us the will to see the best and not the worst that life has to offer. Cheer us that we may overcome our darker moods, calling upon you, Lord, to show us the way back to all that is good and blessed and Christlike. This we ask for Jesus' sake.   Amen.

Our Father . . .

> Let us give thanks to the God and Father of our Lord Jesus Christ, the merciful Father, the God from whom all help comes! He helps us in all our troubles, so that we are able to help others who have all kinds of troubles, using the same help that we ourselves have received from God.
>
> *2 Corinthians 1. 3, 4*

13th MORNING

So we who have found safety with God are greatly encouraged to hold firmly to the hope placed before us. We have this hope as an anchor for our lives. It is safe and sure.

Hebrews 6. 18(b)–19(a)

Hopefulness

Life would be very desolate without hope, Lord. We have our hopes for so many things –
We hope for good health and a happy life for ourselves and our loved ones.

We hope for peace amongst the nations and for safety in our homes.

We hope for fair laws and good Government throughout the world, with an end to tyranny and terrorism.

Hope keeps us going, encourages us and supports us in times of trouble and difficulty. Hope is always there for us to grasp but we let it slip out of our reach.

Lord, we pray that you will always give us the hope we need, for you are the light and hope of the world.   Amen.

The Handicapped

Lord Jesus, as we go about our daily tasks we pray for all those whose lives are restricted through a handicapped body or a retarded mind. When we see examples of the tremendous courage shown by many who have to bear handicaps, we confess with shame, the fuss we make over our own petty trials and tribulations. Keep us watchful to help those weaker than ourselves without being patronising or over attentive, and may we always make time to lend a hand to those who have to live restricted lives. This we ask for Jesus Christ's sake. Amen.

Our Father . . .

Let us be brave, then, and approach God's throne, where there is grace. There we will receive mercy and find grace to help us just when we need it.

Hebrews 4. 16

13th EVENING

To honour the Lord is to hate evil; I hate pride and arrogance, evil ways and false words.

Proverbs 8. 13

Pride

We admit, Lord Jesus, that sometimes we are puffed up and full of our own self-importance. We pretend to know far more than we do. We think that our opinions and decisions are the only right ones. Forgive us Lord for our boastfulness and conceit. Help us to cultivate a will to learn from others who are more experienced or better informed than we are, and the humility to seek advice when we need it. Take our lives and mould them into your ways, that we may walk in your footsteps – the one who showed no pride and yet lived the earthly life of the Son of God.   Amen.

Bad Behaviour

We confess dear Lord that often we behave badly –
From unkind silences and criticism of others;

> Good Lord deliver us.

From slamming doors in anger, using bad language and showing lack of self control.

> Good Lord deliver us.

From pushing others aside in our determination to satisfy our own desires. Good Lord deliver us.
From disrupting the lives of others through our inconsiderateness and lack of understanding.

> Good Lord deliver us.

From forgetting to say we are sorry and refusing to take the blame when we have done wrong.

> Good Lord deliver us.

For these and all our other faults and failings.

> Good Lord deliver us.

Our Father . . .

> I will live a pure life in my house, and will never tolerate evil. I hate the actions of those who turn away from God; I will have nothing to do with them. I will not be dishonest, and will have no dealings with evil.
>
> *Psalm 101. 2–4*

14th MORNING

Our purpose is to do what is right, not only in the sight of the Lord, but also in the sight of man.

2 Corinthians 8. 21

Honesty

Almighty God, you see all that we do and hear all that we say. Shield us from living dishonest lives. Protect us from the petty pilfering which, if un-checked, can grow into stealing and crooked deal-ing. Take from us all thoughts of cheating, whether it be by taking credit for something that is not achieved by our own effort or playing games un-fairly because we want to win. In our daily life guard us from wasting time or mis-using time, so abusing another's trust in us. Help us to see that one of the duties of a Christian is to be a champion of honesty in all its many forms, and fill us with a desire to be upright and reliable in everything.   Amen.

Our Dealings with Others

Lord, you commanded us to love others as much as we love ourselves and yet we find this very hard to put into practice. We pray for opportunities to make up friendships which have been broken; to overcome any dislikes we have which might prove hurtful to others; to offer hospitality to the lonely, the sad and the unloved; to respect the views and feelings of people even if we don't agree with them; to show a helpful spirit without being inquisitive or self-righteous; to behave to others as we would wish them to behave to us. So may we grow daily in love, kindness and thoughtfulness to any who cross our path. This we ask for Jesus's sake.   Amen.

Our Father . . .

> Never tell your neighbour to wait until tomorrow if
> you can help him now. Don't plan anything that
> will hurt your neighbour; he lives beside you trust-
> ing you.
>
> *Proverbs 3. 28, 29*

14th EVENING

Praise the Lord with trumpets. Praise him with harps and lyres. Praise him with drums and dancing. Praise him with harps and flutes. Praise him with cymbals. Praise him with loud cymbals. Praise the Lord, all living creatures! Praise the Lord!

Psalm 150. 3–6

Music and the Arts

Thank You Lord for the great inheritance we enjoy through the efforts of those who have gone before us. We give thanks for past and present authors and illustrators, whose works have upheld the principles of godly living and whose books and articles are read and enjoyed by countless thousands. We give thanks for music and art and all composers and artists, who have used their skills to give us the opportunity to hear and see great works of art and to enjoy magical moments of music, song and dance. We give thanks for actors and actresses on stage and screen and for those who back them up through their talents of design, beauty and production. Lord, we pray that high standards may prevail over evil words and bad influences. This we ask for Jesus Christ's sake.   Amen.

Talents

O God, make us worthy of all your love and kindness to us. Keep us ready and willing to help in spheres where our own particular talents can best be used. Make us humble in any personal success, for we know that we can do but little in our own strength. Preserve us from envy and jealousy of those who find their work, games or past-times easier than we do ourselves, and give us the will to discover our own special gifts in life and to use them in the service of others and to your glory, our Creator and our Friend.   Amen.

Our Father . . .

> For to every person who has something, even more will be given.
>
> *St Matthew 25. 29a*

15th MORNING

Homes are built on the foundation of wisdom and understanding.

Proverbs 24. 3

If you don't punish your son you don't love him. If you do love him you will correct him.

Proverbs 13. 24

Obedience

Guide us Lord to understand that without obedience to reasonable rules and regulations our homes would be places of chaos and unhappiness; our streets would be filled with unruly mobs; our young people would become self-centred and aggressive and life would be frightening and intolerable. Give all parents the will to discipline their children so that they may learn to obey from an early age. Guide adolescents to reject influences which could lead them astray and in your mercy, Lord, forgive us all for our disobedience which undermines our love for you and the keeping of your commandments. This we ask for Jesus' sake. Amen.

Those protecting law and order

We commend to your loving care, almighty Father, those who have dedicated their lives to the difficult task of preserving law and order in this and every land. Be with them as they go about their duties. Protect them from sudden injury and accident, and give them wisdom when they have to make on the spot decisions to guard the lives and safety of others. Help us to help them by being ready and willing to keep the laws of our country, that peace and justice may be preserved and that reverence for you, our Maker and Redeemer, may make this world a happier place in which to live. In the name of Jesus Christ our Lord.   Amen.

Our Father . . .

> We know that the Law is good if it is used as it should be used.
>
> *1 Timothy 1. 8*

15th EVENING

People with a hot temper do foolish things; wiser people remain calm.

Proverbs 14. 17

Bad Temper

When everything seems to be going wrong and our tempers are frayed, help us, Lord, to overcome our rebellious moods. We realise that no one likes us when we are cross and irritable; that often we make so much unnecessary fuss about things which, with a little effort on our part can be put right, while others, who have far heavier crosses to bear than we have, remain cheerful and uncomplaining. When we are at odds with the world help us to see difficulties in their right perspective. Teach us not to get all hot and bothered about the unimportant and passing problems of life but to turn to you, our Lord and Saviour, for peace of heart and mind.   Amen.

Violence in Society

You teach us, Lord, that it is not our task to judge others, especially when we are so quick to forget our own sins and shortcomings. We pray that we may never be responsible for causing hostility which might lead to violence. When violence does erupt we can see that in a very short time anger, jealousy and unreasonable behaviour can turn into an argument resulting in an uncontrollable affray – things are said and done and lives are endangered for unjust and unfair causes. We pray tonight for all who have taken the life of another; who have caused injury to others by their temper or lack of thought; who have treated fellow human beings wrongfully and have caused great suffering to innocent people. Forgive us, Lord, for all our past misdeeds and help us to try at all times to be a good influence on others.   Amen.

Our Father . . .

> Do not go where evil men go. Do not follow the example of the wicked. Don't do it! Keep away from evil! Refuse it and go on your way.
>
> *Proverbs 4. 14, 15*

16th MORNING

> My children, our love should not be just words and talk; it must be true love, which shows itself in action.
>
> *1 John 3. 18*

Sympathy

Lord, you teach us that what we do for others is a way of showing our love for you. Grant that we may not miss opportunities which, if used in the right way, may strengthen our faith and the faith of those we are seeking to serve in your name. We pray that our letter of sympathy may bring comfort to one who is in trouble; the touch, the embrace, the kiss, may assure the disheartened of our concern and friendship; the gift of our money or our worldly goods may encourage and support those who need our help. Forgive us when we have been slack and uncaring, shutting our eyes to the well-being of our neighbours and our fellow men and women. Fill us with a desire to show love and understanding at all times. This we ask for the love of Jesus Christ.   Amen.

Old Age

Oh God, the Father of us all, we pray for those who have grown older and are beginning to find life a burden. Cheer and comfort them as they have to face the limitations of failing eyesight, hardness of hearing or impediment of speech. Surround them with your love when they find it impossible to walk unaided and have to rely on others for their most intimate needs. When we ourselves reach the time when days are long and our work seems finished, give us the grace, heavenly Father, to accept the things we cannot change and to draw ever closer to you, conscious of the great Christian hope of a fuller, richer life in the world to come – a world where there will be no more sorrow or suffering and where we shall be for ever with you the Father of us all.   Amen.

Our Father . . .

> Do not rebuke an older man, but appeal to him as if he were your father. Treat the younger men as your brothers, the older women as mothers, and the younger women as sisters, with all purity.
>
> *1 Timothy 5. 1, 2*

16th EVENING

Keep your faith and a clear conscience. Some men have not listened to their conscience and have made a ruin of their faith.

1 Timothy 1. 19

The Voice of Conscience

Lord, when we look back over the past day, we know that so often, by word and deed we have let you down.

We recall our angry words spoken in the heat of the moment;
Give us the courage Lord to apologise and make friends again.

We remember the thank you we forgot to say or the letter we never wrote;
Give us the grace to express our gratitude however late we may be in doing so.

We think about the promised invitation we gave verbally but never followed up;
Give us the courtesy to fix a firm date.

We recollect the book borrowed which we have never returned;
Give us the will Lord to return it at the earliest opportunity.

We pray that our word may be our bond and that our life may be dedicated to serving you better. Amen.

The Gift of the Holy Spirit

Dear God, the greatest source of all power, we pray that we may be filled with your Holy Spirit.

Help us to grow in goodness that we may overcome evil.

Help us to grow in love that we may become more like you want us to be.

Help us to grow in joyfulness that we may be happy in your service.

Help us to grow in our desire for peace that our worries may be overcome.

Help us to grow in patience that we may be long suffering in our dealings with others.

Help us to grow in kindness that we may hurt no one.

Help us to grow in faithfulness that we may be worthy of another's trust in us.

Help us to grow in meekness that we may never regard ourselves as superior to others.

Help us to grow in self-control that your Holy Spirit may rule our lives as we put our trust in you.   Amen.

Our Father . . .

> But I am telling you the truth: it is better for you that I go away, because if I do not go, the Helper will not come to you. But if I do go away, then I will send him to you.

St John 16. 7

17th MORNING

Everyone who believes in Jesus Christ will have his sins forgiven through the power of his name.

Acts 10. 43(b)

Forgiveness

Forgive us Lord –
For work badly done and jobs unfinished;
For selfish thoughts and wrong motives;
For unkind gossip and disloyalty to friends and neighbours;
For bad temper and an intolerant spirit;
For covetous ways and ungenerous actions;
For criticism of others and not of ourselves;
For jealous thoughts and unworthy opinions;

We know, dear Lord, how often we fail you, but we know too that you came into this world to save sinners. With this great Christian belief, inspire us to do better day by day that we may know the joy of your forgiveness.   Amen.

Social Responsibility

Heavenly Father, in this world of the many homeless and unemployed, the refugees and the outcast, fill us with compassion for all those who need our sympathy and our prayers. As we read of the good Samaritan or the fine example of those Saints who have gone ahead of us, may we be encouraged to do something positive to help. We pray for those whose bed is a cardboard box; whose next meal is taken from the left overs of the better off; who have no home to call their own. Help us to see the urgent need to make real sacrifices ourselves, that others may know that Christians are ready and willing to give what they can to meet the responsibilities laid upon them. This we ask in the name of God our Father.   Amen.

Our Father . . .

> My brothers, what good is it for someone to say that he has faith if his actions do not prove it? Can that faith save him? Suppose there are brothers or sisters who need clothes and don't have enough to eat. What good is there in your saying to them 'God bless you! Keep warm and eat well!' – if you don't give them the necessities of life.
>
> *James 2. 14–16*

17th EVENING

Happy is the person whom God corrects! Do not resent it when he rebukes you. God bandages the wounds he makes; his hand hurts you and his hand heals. Time after time he will save you from harm.

Job 5. 17–19

Disappointment

Heavenly Father, teach us to accept the things we cannot alter and to overcome our disappointments without bitterness and without recrimination. When our lives do not go according to what we have planned and we have to cancel things we had been looking forward to, help us to see that often our ways have not been in accordance with your will. We have succumbed to the lure of the world and have been tempted away from the standards which you have set us. Guide us to turn our disappointments to the advantage of others, that money we might have spent or time we might have wasted may be better used for the welfare of others. This we ask in the name of Jesus Christ, our Lord and Master. Amen.

Right use of Leisure

When we have leisure time, Lord, help us to use it wisely and not just for our own pleasures and pursuits. Give us the vision of a life where people can enjoy each other's company, whether it be by playing games together, listening to music, watching television, sharing a meal or having a chat over the garden fence. Show us ways, dear Lord, of giving up even a small amount of our own leisure time to comfort the sad, to befriend the lonely, to cheer the sick or to visit the house-bound. So, having thought of others, we may feel free to follow our own hobbies and interests without a guilty conscience.   Amen.

Our Father . . .

> Let us conduct ourselves properly, as people who live in the light of day – no orgies or drunkenness, no immorality or indecency, no fighting or jealousy. But take up the weapons of the Lord Jesus Christ, and stop paying attention to your sinful nature and satisfying its desire.
>
> *Romans 13. 13, 14*

18th MORNING

As for you, my brothers, you were called to be free,
but do not let this freedom become an excuse for
letting your physical desires control you. Instead, let
love make you serve one another.

Galations 5. 13

Freedom

We thank you Lord for freedom –

The freedom to choose between right and wrong;
The freedom to laugh when we are happy and to
cry when we are sad;
The freedom to comfort those in distress and the
freedom to help when help is needed;
The freedom to say what we think and the freedom to love our family and friends;
The freedom for children to walk in the streets and
play in safety;

But above all we thank you for that perfect freedom to serve you all our days, no matter what our
circumstances are and no matter how difficult our
situation may be. For even in the depths of despair,
fettered by rules and regulations, imprisoned or
held hostage, we know that we can always pray to
you, our Saviour and our Friend.   Amen.

The Beauty of the World

Open our eyes, Lord, to the loveliness and beauty of this world which you have created. Teach us to reverence the bounty of the earth, the sky and the sea, that we may never use anything you have given us for wrong purposes. As we marvel at the perfection of a tiny baby's hand as it clasps our finger, or the intricate pattern of a spider's web bedecked with morning dew; as we gaze at the majesty of a snow-capped mountain or the sun shimmering on the sea, we worship you our heavenly Father with awe and wonder.   Amen.

Our Father . . .

God looked at everything he had made and he was very pleased.

Genesis 1. 31

18th EVENING

> Watch out and guard yourselves from every kind of greed; because a person's true life is not made up of the things he owns, no matter how rich he may be.
>
> *St Luke 12. 15*

Greed

We are ashamed, Lord, of our greed and avarice. We are ashamed that the poor are exploited that others may grow richer. We are ashamed to confess that our motives in life are centred on a desire to get rather than to give. Help us, Lord, to overcome this selfish and grasping attitude. Stir in us the will to aid those working to alleviate the poverty of the world and to promote justice and generosity. We pray for those who watch their loved ones die of hunger; for those who suffer through lack of education and knowledge and for those who see no way of improving their living conditions. In your mercy, Lord, help us to help them that the peoples of the richer countries of the world may always remember the needs of the less well off, that wrongs may be righted by deeds as well as by words. Amen.

Stewardship

Lord Jesus, you teach us that it is more blessed to give than to receive. Make us worthy stewards of our time, our talents and our earthly possessions. Grant that we may not waste our opportunities to learn and that our time here on earth may be spent profitably – ready to make sacrifices even if this disrupts our own plans. As we discover the gifts you have given us Lord, show us ways of developing them that they may be used for the benefit of the community and not just hidden away and ignored. Increase in us the desire to give what we can of our love, our compassion and our help. This we ask for Jesus' sake.   Amen.

Our Father . . .

> Each one, as a good manager of God's different gifts, must use for the good of others the special gift he has received from God.
>
> *1 Peter 4. 10*

19th MORNING

The Lord's servant must not quarrel. He must be kind towards all, a good and patient teacher, who is gentle as he corrects his opponents, for it may be that God will give them the opportunity to repent and come to know the truth.

2 Timothy 2. 24, 25

Respect

Almighty Father, we pray that we may grow in respect for others. We thank you for the knowledge we gain from teachers, for the skill of inventors and the diligence of researchers and from the words and works of those who have gone before us. Give us respect for all those in authority over us – those elected to govern our country; those who preserve law and order; those who preach the Gospel and those who carry the good news of the Gospel to distant lands. In our daily life help us to grow in respect for those we meet at work or during our leisure time – our parents, our family, our friends, our colleagues in shop or office, factory or workshop. So, as we grow in respect, may we grow in love and reverence for you, Almighty God, that we may appreciate more fully all the love and care you shower upon us day by day.   Amen.

Travellers

Save us, Lord, from an impatient and intolerant spirit when we journey by land, sea or air. Give us the grace to remember that we are not the only ones using the roads, waiting to board a ship or fly in an aircraft. High speed travel brings us opportunities to visit places and people so much more easily and yet, in our negligence and lack of manners, accidents increase and more and more lives are put at risk. When we ourselves are in control of a vehicle, we pray that we may observe speed limits, conform to laws and generally behave in a responsible way. Protect us from the careless minority who drive irresponsibly and take unnecessary risks, that wherever our journeys take us, we may reach our destination safely. This we ask in the name of Christ our Lord and Saviour. Amen.

Our Father . . .

> Love your neighbour as you love yourself. If you love someone, you will never do him wrong; to love, then, is to obey the whole Law.
>
> *Romans 13. 9(c), 10*

19th EVENING

These people are always grumbling and blaming others; they follow their own evil desires; they boast about themselves and flatter others in order to get their own way.

Jude 16

Grumbling

Heavenly Father, when your Son came to live on this earth he accepted all the problems of earthly life without complaint. He accepted the dangers and degradation which he suffered with resolute determination and infinite courage. His trust in you was complete. Help us to cultivate this same implicit trust that when we feel like moaning and groaning, we may turn to you for strength to overcome our complaining moods. Uphold us in our times of discontent, that whatever may happen to us we may not become a burden to others; but, putting our hope and trust in you, we may find strength and courage to face up to difficult situations in the certain belief that you will sustain us, our God and our Redeemer.   Amen.

Discipline

Lord, we pray for discipline –
Discipline to control our appetites in our eating and drinking; In our relationships with others; in our getting and spending; in our desire to satisfy our own pleasures and pursuits; in our quiet times for prayer and Bible reading and in our desire to live a godly life.

Lord, we pray for obedience –
Obedience to our elders and betters; to the laws of our country; to the needs of our family and friends; to the call of duty and to the commandments of God.

Lord, we pray that we may be industrious –
Industrious in our work that we may do a job well; in our efforts to improve our knowledge and endeavours; in our desire to give of our best; in our search for truth and the realisation that without you the purpose of life has been taken from us.   Amen.

Our Father . . .

> Everyone who saw me or heard of me had good things to say about what I had done. When the poor cried out, I helped them; I gave help to orphans who had nowhere to turn. Men who were in deepest misery praised me, and I helped widows find security. I have always acted justly and fairly. I was eyes for the blind and feet for the lame. I was like a father to the poor and took the side of strangers in trouble.
> *Job 29. 11–16*

20th MORNING

A Jew named Apollos was an eloquent speaker and had a thorough knowledge of the Scriptures. He had been instructed in the Way of the Lord and with great enthusiasm he proclaimed and taught correctly the facts about Jesus.

Acts 18. 24, 25

Diligence

Keep us wide awake, Lord, to all the opportunities we may have today to strengthen and show forth our love for you. Make us zealous to follow in your ways without being pious or pretentious. Give us the will to complete tasks well, as though we were doing them for you. Inspire in us diligence not to neglect our daily prayers. Grant that we may never shut you out of our lives, but may always be ready and willing to be messengers of your love, peace, hope, comfort and joy. This we ask for Jesus' sake. Amen.

Natural Resources and Conservation

Thank you Lord for another day to live amidst the variety and beauty of your world. Make us constantly aware that we are but stewards, in our generation, of all that you provide. We realise that if we misuse or over use your earthly provisions just for ourselves, future generations will suffer because of our greed. Lord, we pray that we may heed the advice of experts in the right way to cultivate our crops and garden vegetables, that we may not be responsible for harming the soil or depleting the forests. Increase the concern of everyone that we may overcome the pollution we cause to our seas and rivers and the atmosphere. So may we have a clear conscience that we are trying to do all we can to keep your world clean, unspoilt and beautiful for generations yet unborn.   Amen.

Our Father . . .

> The Lord spoke to Job . . . Were you there when I made the world? If you know so much, tell me about it. Who decided how large it would be? Who stretched the measuring-line over it? Do you know all the answers? What holds up the pillars that support the earth? Who laid the corner-stone of the world?
>
> *Job 38. 4–6*

20th EVENING

> But when the Holy Spirit comes upon you, you will be filled with power, and you will be witnesses for me in Jerusalem, in all Judaea and Samaria, and to the ends of the earth.
>
> *Acts 1. 8*

Timid Witness

Strengthen our resolve, Lord, to stand up for what is right and to fight against evil;

to respect the law, so setting a good example in obedience and duty;

to uphold family life and to pray for those with broken homes;

to show courage that endures in the face of opposition, suffering and pain;

to increase in truthfulness through our words and deeds;

to control our tempers and our feelings when we are provoked and treated as unbelievers.

Above all Lord, strengthen our resolve to increase in moral courage and our witness for you, knowing that you are our refuge and strength and a very present help in trouble, our Saviour and our Lord. Amen.

Teachers

O Loving Father and Divine Teacher forgive
parents when they are unkind and unloving to
their children;
when teachers lose patience with unruly and undisciplined pupils in their classes;
when anger takes the place of reasoning and
persuasion;
when our homes and places of learning are dis-
rupted by the unchecked trouble makers.

Dear Lord, we pray that love and common sense
may rule in our homes; that discipline and encouragement may prevail in our schools and colleges;
that forgiveness and understanding may be shown
to all who find it hard to obey rules and regulations. Above all, we pray that those entrusted with
the opportunity of helping to mould the mind of a
child, may turn to you for guidance and wisdom
in this supreme duty of building lives on a firm
Christian foundation.   Amen.

Our Father . . .

> Go then, to all peoples everywhere and make them
> my disciples; baptize them in the name of the Father,
> the Son and the Holy Spirit, and teach them to obey
> everything I have commanded you. And I will be
> with you always, to the end of the age.
>
> *St Matthew 28. 19, 20*

21st MORNING

All of you must put on the apron of humility to serve one another; for the scripture says 'God resists the proud, but shows favour to the humble'. Humble yourselves, then, under God's mighty hand, so that he will lift you up in his own good time.

1 Peter 5. 5, 6

Humility

Lord Jesus Christ, we thank you for your teaching that the humble shall receive your praise and that those who become great are those who accept the cloak of humility. Guard us from self-righteousness and make us willing to accept fair criticism without complaint, that your ways may become our ways and your laws our laws. If pride should creep into our lives, give us the strength to overcome it, knowing that we ourselves can achieve but little without your blessing, our Lord and our Saviour. Amen.

True Values

Root out of our lives, almighty God, the transient
values of daily living;
the love of money and possessions;
the longing for power and prestige which sometimes goes before a fall;
the covetous spirit which makes us dissatisfied
with our life.

Open our eyes to the love we receive from others;
the sympathy and compassion they show us in our
sorrows and disappointments;
the happiness we can share with them when things
go right and we have good news.

Above all else, help us to keep you and your love
for us in the centre of our lives, that we may grow
in contentment and fulfilment as we endeavour to
uphold your values.   Amen.

Our Father . . .

> No longer, then do we judge anyone by human
> standards. Even if at one time we judged Christ
> according to human standards, we no longer do so.
> When anyone is joined to Christ, he is a new being;
> the old is gone, the new has come.
>
> *2 Corinthians 5. 16, 17*

21st EVENING

Fear the Lord and act carefully, because the Lord our God does not tolerate fraud or partiality or the taking of bribes.

2 Chronicles 19. 7

Lack of Tolerance for Others

Almighty God, there are some people whom we meet in life whom we find difficult. At school or college it is invariably the bullies who annoy us with their overbearing manner and tormenting ways. Then, as we go out into the world we come into contact with the knowalls and the shirkers, the cheats and the tricksters, the hooligans and the drug addicts. Heavenly Father, we know that we too have many faults and failings, and we confess our sins and pray for your forgiveness; we pray too for all those who show lack of regard for others by what they say and do. We ask you to guide everyone into the Christian way of life where love and kindness and caring overcome all feelings of lust, hatred, disrespect and unchari-tableness. Hear our prayer and let our cry come unto you. Amen.

Relationships

Thank you, Lord, for all those who uphold truth with integrity and who are prepared to speak up for the underdog, protecting the weak from stronger adversaries.

Thank you, Lord, for all those whose courage is so great that they can inspire others to remain undaunted in the face of danger.

Thank you, Lord, for the unselfish love of those who encourage and support us in life's dark valleys and stormy waters.

Thank you, Lord, for those in positions of responsibility who shun the trivial and fight to make freedom a reality.

We pray that we may increase our efforts to follow in the footsteps of those who have won the hearts of others through their dedicated service to you. This we ask for Christ's sake.   Amen.

Our Father . . .

> A warning given by an experienced person to some-one willing to listen is more valuable than gold rings or jewellery made of the finest gold.
>
> *Proverbs 25. 12*

22nd MORNING

No one can please God without faith, for whoever comes to God must have faith that God exists and rewards those who seek him.

Hebrews 11. 6

Faith

Lord, make our trust in you complete. We confess that our faith at times is shallow and wavering. In our doubts and disbelief we pray that you will uphold us and assure us of your presence. Strengthen us as we recall the Gospel stories of those who showed their belief in you – the four friends of the paralytic man; the raising of Lazarus and the healing of the lepers, were but a few of the miracles you performed which filled the watching crowds with amazement. Lord, give us a firm and resolute faith that by our witness others may come to trust you as the Saviour of our souls.   Amen.

Sudden Disaster

Lord, there are things we cannot understand:
the ending of a wonderful life caused by a drunken driver;
the heartbreak of the sudden death of a loved one;
the fatal illness of a little child;
the earthquake, hurricane or flooding engulfing hundreds of people;
the carelessness of others which can lead to great loss of life;

Help us, Lord, that we may be able to accept the disasters we cannot understand; not dwelling on the darkness of death, but praying that we too may be fit to enter into the Kingdom of Heaven when our earthly life is over and our work is done.   Amen.

Our Father . . .

> Leave all your worries with him, because he cares for you.
>
> *1 Peter 5. 7*

22nd EVENING

Don't argue with someone for no reason when he
has never done you any harm.

Proverbs 3. 30

Quarrelling

Forgive us, loving Father, for the times when we
have sown discord –

Forgive us for the people we have hurt by disa-
greeing with them in an arrogant or hostile way;
Forgive us if we have fallen out with those we
love;
Forgive us for being quarrelsome and so causing
unnecessary trouble to our family, our friends, our
neighbours or our country;

Help us to realise that a cross word can lead to an
argument; an argument can lead to a misunderstanding and this in turn could lead to strife. Make
us repentant, Lord, and grant that in our dealings
with others we may grow in kindness and toler-
ance, living our lives cheerfully and without complaint, so helping others to be happy and content
too.   Amen.

World Peace

Heavenly Father, we ask your blessing on the nations of the world. We pray for friendship between peoples of other lands, that rivalry and self-interest may give way to harmony and mutual trust, and that hatred and brutality may be transformed into love and kindness. We pray that the more powerful larger nations may not interfere with the ideals and aspirations of the smaller nations and we ask your help in overcoming tyranny and oppression. We pray that dictators may be overthrown and world peace may be firmly established on the foundations of justice and conciliation. If, after exhaustive negotiations war cannot be averted, then Lord, inspire us to fight for justice that the world may see that evil cannot be allowed to prevail, and that those fighting to uphold the right may be victorious in establishing lasting peace to the benefit of all mankind. Amen.

Our Father . . .

> Do everything possible on your part to live in peace with everybody.
>
> *Romans 12. 18*

23rd MORNING

. . .Be an example for the believers in your speech, your conduct, your love, faith and purity.

1 Timothy 4. 12

Purity

Preserve us, Lord, from all the evils and temptations of this world. When others try to influence us to do wrong things, strengthen our resolve to follow in the ways of purity and decency. Drive from us all unclean thoughts and desires, that our eyes may not linger on anything which might rouse lustful thoughts in our minds. Keep us from immoral living and from failing to take a stand against wrong practices. Protect us, Lord, when the devil tries to lure us from your way and keep us firm and constant in our desire to live pure and undefiled lives.   Amen.

The Terminally Ill

Loving Father, pour out your Holy Spirit on all those whose lives are drawing to a close through incurable illnesses, accident or old age. Forgive those who have allowed drugs, smoking or alcohol to master their wills, so shortening their days on earth. Bless those who have been stricken with an illness for which there is no known cure and those who have been seriously injured by sudden violence or misadventure. To those in pain and suffering bring relief; to the penitent bring forgiveness and to the frustrated peace. So grant to all those who are terminally ill grace to accept the promise of a far better life beyond, where there will be no more suffering or pain. This we ask for the sake of Jesus Christ who, in his great mercy, died for each one of us.   Amen.

Our Father . . .

> You have been raised to life with Christ, so set your hearts on the things that are in heaven, where Christ sits on his throne at the right-hand side of God. Keep your minds fixed on things there, not on things here on earth.
>
> *Colossians 3. 1, 2*

23rd EVENING

> But God has shown us how much he loves us – it was while we were still sinners that Christ died for us! By His death we are now put right with God; how much more, then, will we be saved by him from God's anger!
>
> *Romans 5. 8, 9*

Sinners

Forgive us, heavenly Father –

For the times when we have broken your laws and disobeyed your commandments;
For the times we have blamed others for our own misdeeds;
For the times when we have not been strictly honest in what we have said and done.

We acknowledge that we demand immediate attention while others have to wait. We are conceited and self-sufficient. We ignore appeals for caring, shutting our eyes to those crying out for help, and sadly we confess that sometimes we forget all about you and your love for us. Help us, Lord to improve in goodness and right living and please forgive us for our past sins. We pray for your pardon and mercy as we resolve to live more godly lives in your service, the One who died upon the Cross to save us from our sins.   Amen.

Neighbours

Thank You God –

for those who are ready to listen to troubles and to share the burden of sorrow;
for those who will help when another pair of hands is needed;
for those who spread happiness and contentment, looking for the best in life;
for those who show courtesy and thoughtfulness at home, at work or in their daily round of duty;
for those who put others before themselves;
for those who give what they can to help solve the problems of evil;

And above all, for those who show their love for you by making time to be kind.   Amen.

Our Father . . .

> You will be doing the right thing if you obey the law of the Kingdom, which is found in the scripture, 'Love your neighbour as you love yourself.'
>
> *James 2. 8*

. . .Whoever shares with others should do it generously; whoever has authority should work hard; whoever shows kindness to others should do it cheerfully.

Romans 12. 8

Cheerfulness

Loving Lord, we pray that as we go out to face life today you will give us –

A hopeful outlook that we may encourage others;

A lively interest that we may put our highest endeavour into everything we do;

A happy smile that we may overcome the worries and burdens of life;

A cheerful courage which will bring comfort and gladden the hearts of those we meet;

A ready acceptance, in the face of adversity, by putting our trust in heavenly things;

Inspiration that others may see in us something of our love for you our Lord and Master.   Amen.

Angels

Lord, as holy men and women touch and influence our lives for good, so we believe that angels surround us, guarding and guiding us in our going out and coming in. We remember the angels of long ago who in the Gospel story appeared to Mary and Joseph, to Elizabeth and Zechariah, and to many others who obeyed your call. Keep us alert and watchful to recognise your holy messengers in whatever form they may come, and as we worship you in the company of the countless heavenly host, we praise and thank you for angels and archangels and all the company of Heaven.

Our Father . . .

> Jacob dreamt that he saw a stairway reaching from earth to heaven, with angels going up and coming down on it. And there was the Lord standing beside him.
>
> *Genesis 28. 12. 13*

24th EVENING

Remember the Lord in everything you do, and he
will show you the right way.

Proverbs 3. 6

Tactlessness

Save us, Lord, from tactlessness and discourtesy,
from saying hurtful things and from pushing ourselves forward; from black looks, bad temper and
a perverse spirit. As we strive to improve our
characters, teach us to be sensitive – ready to show
courtesy and humility with a joyful countenance
and a generosity which always seeks the good in
all things and people. Help us to face the inevitable
without grumbling and never to let the sun go
down on an unresolved quarrel or a sullen silence.
This we ask for Jesus' sake.   Amen.

Matrimonial Problems

We bring into your presence, Lord, all those who are faced with troubles in their married life, and we specially think of ...... at this time. We pray that every married couple may learn that two of the secrets of a happy marriage are to give as well as take and to allow oneself to be loved as well as to love. Strengthen the wills of those at present in difficulties that they may not give up hope in resolving them. We recall, Lord, the marriage in Cana of Galilee where you changed the water into wine and in the same way we pray that, as we share our sorrows and problems with you, the simple everyday things of life may be enriched and become channels of forgiveness, patience and love in whatever circumstances we find ourselves. This we ask for your love's sake.   Amen.

Our Father . . .

> Be tolerant with one another and forgive one another whenever any of you has a complaint against some-one else. You must forgive one another just as the Lord has forgiven you. And to all these qualities add love, which binds all things together in perfect unity.
> *Colossians 3. 13. 14*

25th MORNING

But if you endure suffering even when you have
done right, God will bless you for it. It was to this
that God called you, for Christ himself suffered for
you and left you an example, so that you would
follow in his steps.

1 Peter 2. 20, 21

A Good Influence

Merciful God, we pray that as your disciples went
about doing good, preaching the Good News of
the Gospel and living selfless lives, we too may
grow in understanding and commitment to your
teaching. Fill us with the desire to capture something of your great love for all, that our influence
amongst those we meet may be worthy of our
discipleship. Help us to keep your commandments,
and to remember at all times that we are your
servants, trying to do our part, however small, to
further your Kingdom here on earth.   Amen.

Women, Wives and Mothers

Lord, we beseech you to bless all women everywhere. As we begin our work today we think of the women who are tired and lonely, sad or overwhelmed with daily chores. We think of wives and mothers who have the great privilege of making a home and bringing up their children. We know that life can be very demanding and unrewarding in the cleaning and cooking, washing and ironing and all the other jobs around the house. We think of girls and younger women who are faced with the choice of finding the right lifetime partner. We remember especially those faithful and devoted ones who care for the handicapped and ageing relatives with such love and dedication. Lord, bless all women and grant them strength and patience to help build up a firm foundation for home and family life in this and every land.   Amen.

Our Father . . .

> The older women must teach what is good, in order to train the younger women to love their husbands and children, to be self-controlled and pure, and to be good housewives.
>
> *Titus 2 3(part)–5*

25th EVENING

> For the love of money is a source of all kinds of evil. Some have been so eager to have it that they have wandered away from the faith and have broken their hearts with many sorrows.
>
> *1 Timothy 6. 10*

The Love of Money

Lord, we get and spend and still we want more. However much of this world's good things we have, there are many of us who are never satisfied. The acquisitive spirit takes over our lives and this in turn spoils the enjoyment of life. When we feel like this Lord, turn our thoughts to the poor and those who never have enough. Then Lord, in your mercy, show us how to be merciful too. We pray that through our generosity we may be instrumental in giving sight to the blind, hearing to the deaf, food to the hungry and hope to the faint-hearted. All this we ask in your name that in some small way we may share in relieving the sufferings of the world.   Amen.

Inhospitality

Pardon us, heavenly Father, when we are not as polite and welcoming as we ought to be; the unexpected guest arrives just as we are about to watch our favourite television programme or listen to the radio; the telephone rings as we sit down to a hot meal after a tiring day; the doorbell can be equally annoying when we are doing something we want to do. Our patience is tried and we feel cross. But we know that people matter. A welcoming smile or making time for a chat bring comfort and a feeling of being wanted to those who have no one to talk to them. Lord, please help us to be more like you want us to be. You were never too tired or busy to listen to others and to talk to them. We are ashamed of our selfishness and impatience and pray that in our daily living we must always try to put you first, others second and ourselves last.   Amen.

Our Father . . .

> Keep on loving one another as Christian brothers. Remember to welcome strangers in your homes. There were some who did that and welcomed angels without knowing it.
>
> *Hebrews 13. 1, 2*

26th MORNING

> The Lord will guard you; he is by your side to
> protect you. The sun will not hurt you during the
> day, nor the moon during the night. The Lord will
> protect you from all danger; he will keep you safe.
> He will protect you as you come and go now and
> for ever.
>
> *Psalm 121. 5–8*

Protection

We give thanks to you, heavenly Father, for the
gift of another day, and we pray that you will
strengthen us to fight against all the evils of the
world, the flesh and the devil. Grant us your
protection that we may turn from everything
which is not according to your Holy will. Protect
us from greed and covetousness; from spending
beyond our means; from eating and drinking to
excess; from abusing our bodies by the taking of
drugs or indulging in unlawful sexual relationships. O God, we accept that trying to follow the
Christian way of life does not shield us from
sorrow or misfortune, but we know too that with
you by our side, we can face life in the sure hope
that you will watch over us and protect us all our
days.   Amen.

Men, Husbands and Fathers

Lord, we beseech you to bless all men everywhere. We think of boys and adolescents and pray that as they grow to manhood they may increase in wisdom and consideration for others. Guide fathers to instruct their children in the discipline of daily life, that parents may realise that their good example is all important to the children entrusted to their care. We pray that single men may never take unfair advantage of women and that married men may be faithful and loving to their wives. Turn the hearts of all to follow in your ways Lord, that we may be led into the paths of unity, sound judgement and love. This we ask for the sake of Jesus Christ.   Amen.

Our Father . . .

The Lord corrects those he loves, as a father corrects a son of whom he is proud. Happy is the man who becomes wise – who gains understanding.

Proverbs 3. 12, 13

26th EVENING

Do not steal or cheat or lie.

Leviticus 19. 11

Stealing

Guard us Lord from the desire to obtain anything under false pretences and from taking things which do not belong to us.

We acknowledge that:
We casually borrow something and do not bother to return it;
We take a longer break from our work than we are entitled to;
We speak harshly or critically of someone else, so undermining another person's character;
We steal someone's innocence by leading them astray;

We remember in our prayers tonight all those known and unknown to us who have been the victims of burglary, blackmail, fraud, kidnap, rape, larceny, murder and all other forms of theft.

We pray too for all those who have broken your commandment not to steal. Forgive them and us Lord, and strengthen our resolve to grow in honest dealing as we strive to live upright lives. Amen.

Child Abuse

We ask your blessing, heavenly Father, on all children. As they are born into the world and you entrust them to our care, grant that we may be worthy of their love and dependence on us. Keep them from harm both physically and mentally. Where there is cruelty in the home protect them. Where there is quarrelling bring understanding, and where there is unkindness bring love. So may all those responsible for the welfare of children, in any way, heed your words to suffer the children to come to you and never to deprive them of learning about you, their Lord and Master. Amen.

Our Father . . .

> So Jesus called a child, made him stand in front of them, and said 'I assure you that, unless you change and become like children, you will never enter the Kingdom of Heaven. . . .If anyone should cause one of these little ones to lose his faith in me, it would be better for that person to have a large millstone tied round his neck and be drowned in the deep sea.'
> *Matthew 18. 2, 3 & 6*

27th MORNING

Happy are those whose greatest desire is to do what God requires; God will satisfy them fully!

St Matthew 5. 6

Happiness

Help us, Lord, to spread a little happiness as we journey through life. There is always so much to be sad about and this can make us forget to rejoice and be glad. We hear of unhappy marriages and unhappy homes, but there are countless families who find great joy in just being together. We read in our newspapers and hear on the media of violence and neglect, cruelty and abuse, and yet stories of gallantry and unselfishness, kindness and love, often take second place. Help us to be on the lookout for inspiring and uplifting deeds and to speak a word of praise whenever we can. So may we show a firm trust in our great Christian heritage, trying at all times to look on the bright side of life. Amen.

Holidays

Thank you, God, for times to relax – times to take our ease surrounded by the beauty and variety of the seasons.

Thank you for Summer sunshine and the songs of the birds; for swimming and sailing and fresh sea breezes, fishing and riding and outdoor games.

Thank you for Autumn and leaves changing colour; stately homes to visit and crops to bring in;
Thank you for Winter and skiing and skating – Christmas and parties, the fireside and books.

Thank you for Spring, new life and green meadows; flowers and blossom and the humming of bees;
Thank you for freedom, for silence and wonder as we ponder anew at Your wonderful world; for rest and refreshment which holidays bring us, for God in our hearts and the love of the Lord.   Amen.

Our Father . . .

> The Lord is my shepherd; I have everything I need. He lets me rest in fields of green grass and leads me to quiet pools of fresh water. He gives me new strength. He guides me in the right paths as he has promised.

> *Psalm 23. 1–3*

27th EVENING

So then, stand firm and steady. Keep busy always in your work for the Lord, since you know that nothing you do in the Lord's service is ever useless.

1 Corinthians 15. 58

Endurance

Heavenly Father, we acknowledge that we are not always as conscientious as we ought to be. We put things off because we don't want to do them or don't like doing them. We give up before we have even tried and make excuses when we know that we should persevere in getting a job finished. We pray tonight for all who live and work in stressful circumstances. Those who have to bear the burdens of others as well as their own; those who have to suffer pain and persecution; those who find it hard to overcome their faults and failings. This we ask in the name of Jesus Christ, our Lord and Saviour. Amen.

Confidence

O God, fill us with boldness that we may meet the demands of life with a brave heart and without complaint. When the path of life is dark and difficult and the right way seems the hardest way, be with us Lord. May our footsteps never falter, and when we reach the point of no return, give us courage to go forward, fixing our eyes upon the Cross, where we can see the supreme example of true courage and confidence in the sacrifice of our beloved Master, Jesus Christ.   Amen.

Our Father . . .

> In union with Christ and through our faith in him, we have the boldness to go into God's presence with all confidence. I beg you then not to be discouraged.
>
> *Ephesians 3. 12, 13(a)*

28th MORNING

Remember that I have commanded you to be determined and confident; Don't be afraid or discouraged, for I, the Lord your God, am with you wherever you go.

Joshua 1. 9

Partings

Almighty God, we pray for those from whom for a time we are parted –

Children and young people who have left home to attend boarding school or college;
Friends and relations whose work has taken them to another district or country;
Employers and employees who travel the world to promote business and commerce;
Men and women serving in the Forces at home and in distant lands;
Older folk who spend their days in rest homes and are often cut off by distance from those they love.

Our nearest and dearest who have gone to be with you in Paradise.

We ask your blessing, heavenly Father, on the lonely and sad, those far from home and those feeling isolated in strange surroundings. Bless them all as we entrust them to your care and keeping.   Amen.

Fear

Dear Lord, we ask your help to overcome our fears – fears which can grip us and haunt us, so spoiling our lives and undermining our faith. Strengthen us to fight the unfounded fears which make us timid and anxious, and the superstitions which influence us to make wrong decisions and not to use our powers of reasoning. Steel our hearts against alarming thoughts which can be transmitted to the minds of others, and the panic which gives rise to fright and terror. Teach us, Lord, to face all our fears bravely, knowing that you are always there to reassure us if we put our trust in you.   Amen.

Our Father . . .

Tell everyone who is discouraged, be strong and don't be afraid, God is coming to your rescue.

Isaiah 35. 4

28th EVENING

The Spirit has given us life; he must also control our lives.

Galatians 5. 25

Good Conduct

Hear us, Lord, as we pray –

That all children may obey their parents and teachers within the school and family circle;

That young people may show respect in their relationships with others both at college and in their work;

That married couples may honour and uphold the vows they made together on their wedding day;

That the middle-aged, by their example and witness to God, may influence for good all those committed to their care;

That those who are older may be ready to give wise adivce from their own experiences in life without being dogmatic or self-righteous;

That we may all love, honour and obey God, trying, at all times and in all places, to shine as lights for him, our Father and our King.   Amen.

Manners

We confess, Lord, that we are guilty of looking askance when others do not show compassion or consideration, and yet we ourselves are guilty of bad manners and lack of thought. We forget to give a helping hand, to those confined to their homes caring for ageing parents or shouldering the responibility of bringing up young children single-handed. We drive our cars without stopping to let another driver out at a difficult junction, and we are quite content to see our own needs met as long as our plans don't have to be altered for the sake of helping others. Teach us to see, Lord, that good manners are a must in the building of a Christlike character, and that if we wish to grow in the Christian faith, the needs of others must come first as we strive to live as you would have us live. Amen.

Our Father . . .

> Do not be fooled. Bad companions ruin good character. Come back to your right senses and stop your sinful ways.
>
> *1 Corinthians 15. 33*

When things are going well for you, be glad, and when trouble comes just remember: God sends both happiness and trouble, you never know what is going to happen next.

Ecclesiastes 7. 14

When people are happy, they smile, but when they are sad they look depressed.

Proverbs 15. 13

A Sense of Humour

Give us a sense of humour Lord, and a heart to rejoice in the fun of life; a ready wit and a happy smile that others may sing and be glad. Give us a love of the good and the true; that our jokes may not hurt or our laughter harm, and fill our souls with the joy of your love that the earth may rejoice in the Lord.   Amen.

Sportsmanship

Heavenly Father, teach us to play the game in our dealings with others. Give us an open mind that we may make fair and right decisions, never knowingly cheating either in business or in sport. Keep us from unnecessary arguments on decisions made by referees and those in authority, that we may try, at all times, to be fair to those who oppose us, and willing to show sportsmanship even when we are on the losing side. We pray that through our behaviour others may see in us glimpses of your love of truth, strength of character and steadfastness of purpose. This we ask for your love's sake.   Amen.

Our Father . . .

> Every athlete in training submits to strict discipline, in order to be crowned with a wreath that will not last; but we do it for one that will last for ever.
>> *1 Corinthians 9. 25*

> An athlete who runs in a race cannot win the prize unless he obeys the rules.
>> *2 Timothy 2. 5*

29th EVENING

Every test that you have experienced is the kind that normally comes to people. But God keeps his promise and he will not allow you to be tested beyond your power to remain firm; at the time you are put to the test, he will give you the strength to endure it, and so provide you with a way out.

1 Corinthians 10. 13

Temptation

O God, our loving Father, we pray that whenever temptation crosses our path we may have the resolution to resist it. We remember before you all those who are tempted to produce or read pornography; those who are influenced to take drugs and those who supply and sell them; people who refuse to uphold the moral standards of your world and who drag others down to stealing, adultery, rape, violent crime and even to murder. We confess that when we are confronted by temptations we are not always as quick as we ought to be to condemn them. Cleanse us God in all our thoughts, words and deeds that we may strive not to defile our characters by sinful and ungodly living. Amen.

God's Commandments

Heavenly Father, you have given us a set of rules for living but we find it very difficult not to break them. We have turned your world into a place where your standards seem almost unattainable, and yet we know that your commandments hold the secret to a world where love for you and for one another is supreme. We pray for a deeper, more lasting spirit of loving, caring and sharing throughout your universe, that sin and wickedness may be cast away and love, joy and peace may unite us all in the bonds of fellowship and understanding. This we ask for the sake of Him who died for us, Jesus Christ our Lord. Amen.

Our Father . . .

> Keep me from going the wrong way, and in your goodness teach me your law.
>
> *Psalm 119. 29*

> I will eagerly obey your commands because you will give me more understanding.
>
> *Psalm 119. 32*

The Lord said 'There is a large harvest, but few workers to gather it in. Pray to the owner of the harvest that he will send out workers to gather in his harvest.'

St Luke 10. 2

The Unfolding of the Good News

O God, our Father, all mankind is crying out for your love and help. We confess that our witness is so timid when it should be bold; the words which we should speak, proclaiming our trust in you, are silenced by a lack of assurance as to what we should say; our good intentions are overcome by our shallow efforts to increase our knowledge of you. Forgive us, God, for our unworthiness to extol You and give us that resolution and courage, that will inspire others to turn to you, putting you in the centre of their lives as they seek to find the way to a richer, better life here on earth.   Amen.

The Church in the World

Almighty God, keep ever before us the vision of a world where there is harmony between the nations. Give courage and wisdom to all who have dedicated their lives to your service in this and other lands. Help us all to see that your laws are central to our civilisation and turn our thoughts away from dogmatic faults and trendy fashionable causes so that your Gospel may be preached in a way which is understood by ordinary people. We thank you for guidance in the past, encouragement in the present and hope for the future, and we pray for the strengthening of the bonds of fellowship and peace between Christian people and those of other creeds. This we ask in the Name of the Father, the Son and the Holy Spirit.   Amen.

Our Father . . .

> Remember how great is God's power; he is the greatest teacher of all. He has always been praised for what he does; you also must praise him.
>
> *Job 36. 22 & 24*

30th EVENING

Make good use of every opportunity you have. Your speech should always be pleasant and interesting and you should know how to give the right answer to everyone.

Colossians 4. 5(b), 6

Boredom

Give us attentive minds, Lord, and keep us alert and diligent in our daily living. Take from us the dejected and disinterested attitude which makes us dull and boring. Instead, stimulate us to look around and see our life as an opportunity to increase in our knowledge of things and people, and to accept the challenge to live our lives to a high moral standard on our journey Godwards. When we feel rebellious and think of days we are spending in a dull, humdrum routine, teach us to appreciate new discoveries and inventions, which bring variety and pleasure into our homes, and to be thankful, Lord, that you have provided so much from which our generation can benefit.   Amen.

All Living Things

We thank you, Lord, for your creation:

For buds bursting into glorious flowers and blossom;
For milk from cows and eggs from hens;
For wool from sheep and fish from the sea;
For corn in the fields and bread to eat;
For dogs and cats and all our pets.

As we marvel at your handiwork we pray for gardeners, farmers, veterinary surgeons, foresters and all who tend to the needs of living things. Uphold their love for everything they hold dear, that nothing may be wasted or ill-treated as we praise and glorify the beauty of your living world.   Amen.

Our Father . . .

> The whole world stands in awe of the great things that you have done. Your deeds bring shouts of joy from one end of the earth to the other.
>
> *Psalm 65. 8*

> Don't worry about anything but in all your prayers
> ask God for what you need, always asking him with
> a thankful heart. And God's peace, which is far
> beyond human understanding, will keep your hearts
> and minds safe in union with Christ Jesus.
>
> *Philippians 4. 6, 7*

Inner Peace

Lord, whatever may befall us through illness,
accident, unexpected happenings, loss or bereave-
ment, help us to trust in your everlasting care.
Teach us to accept the things we fight against and
to face difficulties and troubles with an unflinching
faith in you. That strengthened by your love and
conscious of your unseen presence supporting us,
we may remain calm and tranquil in the knowledge that you will help us to overcome the stresses
and strains of life.   Amen.

Lack of Love

We pray for all those living in the dark places of the world, where love is lacking and where people have to live their lives in fear and loneliness with no one to support and encourage them. Be with those in prison and disgrace; the friendless and sad; the homeless and unemployed; the victims of situations over which they have no control; the unloved and abused; those being held hostage and those called upon to suffer for things they have never done. Use us Lord, to be messengers of your love that we may bring hope to the despairing and friendship to the friendless. This we ask for your love's sake.   Amen.

Our Father . . .

> Remember those who are in prison, as though you were in prison with them. Remember those who are suffering as though you were suffering as they are.
>
> *Hebrews 13. 3*

31st EVENING

When I lie down, I go to sleep in peace, you, alone,
O Lord, keep me perfectly safe.

Psalm 4. 8

Sleep and Rest

Grant us Lord to relax our minds; sleep to refresh
our bodies; peace to restore our faith and the gift
of the Holy Spirit to uplift our souls, that our lives
may be filled and recharged with love for you. We
pray that the sun may never go down on our anger
and that in all our dealings with others we may
learn to forgive and forget; to love and not to hate;
to help and not to hinder. So, putting you above
all else, grant us the peace which passes human
understanding and the rest which will restore us to
meet the demands of another day. This we ask for
Christ's sake.   Amen.

Eternal Life

Almighty God, you have promised a place in heaven to all those who love you with all their heart, soul, mind and strength. Guide us in your ways, that as we face the difficulties and challenges of this mortal life we may grow in our reverence for you and our trust in you. Teach us to be faithful to your commandments and constant in your service, that when the call comes for us to leave this earthly life, we may be worthy of a place in your eternal Kingdom. This we ask for the sake of Jesus Christ, your Son, our pattern and our King.   Amen.

Our Father . . .

> For God loved the world so much that he gave his only Son, so that everyone who believes in him may not die but have eternal life.
>
> *St John 3. 16*

SUBJECT INDEX